TO ACCOMPANY
AIR PILOT'S MANUAL - VOLUME 7

Questions, Answers & Explanations

EASA PPL Revision Papers

Communications

Written and illustrated by
Helena B A Hughes

POOLEYS
Air Pilot Publishing

STOP PRESS – New UK CAA PPL e-Exams - The UK CAA are introducing new PPL e-Exams from October 2020. Rather than using paper exam sets, all the exams will now be taken online under controlled conditions. They will, however, still be taken at your flying school and under the supervision of an approved individual. Please note that the syllabus has not changed. By reading the Air Pilots Manuals and other reading materials mentioned in the books, and by testing yourself with the following test papers, you will be ready to undertake these new exams. The CAA has issued guidance for students taking these exams and this can be found by searching online for CAP1903G.

Copyright © 2020 Pooleys Flight Equipment Limited.

EASA Private Pilot Licence Aeroplane & Helicopter Questions, Answers & Explanations – Communications

ISBN 978-1-84336-202-9

First Edition published February 2014
Reprinted June 2014
Reprint February 2016
Reprint January 2017
Revised Edition July 2017
Revised Edition September 2020

Origination by Pooleys Flight Equipment Limited.

Published by Pooleys Flight Equipment Ltd

Elstree Aerodrome
Hertfordshire WD6 3AW
Tel: +44(0)20 8953 4870
Web: www.pooleys.com
Email: sales@pooleys.com

AUTHOR

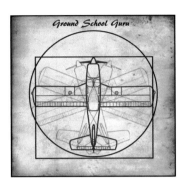

Helena B A Hughes

Helena Hughes was born into an aviation household, having her first informal "flying lesson" at the age of four. Her late father David was a flying instructor and also flew corporate jets. On leaving University Helena obtained her PPL. Shortly afterwards she started work in Air Traffic Control at London Luton Airport earning her Controllers Licence in 1990. Helena continues to be an operational Air Traffic Control Officer and is currently posted to Swanwick working "Thames Radar", "Luton Radar" and "Heathrow Special"; she is involved in controller training as both an Instructor and Assessor. Helena holds a fixed wing CPL/IR and has been a flying instructor since 1996. She also holds a PPL(H) and is a Radio Telephony and Air/Ground Examiner.

Helena would like to thank: Mrs. Brenda "Bedda" Hughes; Mr. Andrew Temple of Solent Flight Ltd; A Vrancken and H Ewing

INTRODUCTION

This book is intended as an aid to revision and examination preparation for those studying for the grant of an EASA PPL. Ideally its use should follow a period of self or directed study to consolidate the knowledge acquired and identify any areas of weakness prior to attempting the PPL examinations themselves.

The questions and answers in this publication are designed to reflect those appearing in the current examination papers and are set out in a representative format. No attempt has been made to replicate any actual examination paper.

Blank answer sheets are provided at the end of the book which may be photocopied to enable multiple attempts at each exam.

EDITORS

Dorothy Saul-Pooley LLB(Hons) FRAeS

Dorothy holds an ATPL (A) and a CPL (H), and is both an instructor and examiner on aeroplanes and an instructor on helicopters. She is Head of Training for a school dedicated to running Flight Instructor courses at Shoreham. She is also a CAA Flight Instructor Examiner. In addition, having qualified as a solicitor in 1982, Dorothy acted for many years as a consultant specialising in aviation and insurance liability issues, and has lectured widely on air law and insurance issues. This highly unusual combination of qualifications led to her appointment as Honorary Solicitor to the Guild of Air Pilots and Navigators (GAPAN). Dorothy is a Fellow of the Royal Aeronautical Society, first Chairman of the GAPAN Instructor Committee, and past Chairman of the Education & Training Committee. She has just completed her term of office as the Master for the year 2014-15 of the Honourable Company of Air Pilots (formerly GAPAN). She is also Chairman of the Professional Flying Instructors Association. In 2003 she was awarded the Jean Lennox Bird Trophy for her contribution to aviation and support of Women in Aviation and the BWPA (British Women Pilots Association). In 2013 Dorothy was awarded the prestigious Master Air Pilots Certificate by GAPAN. A regular contributor to seminars, conferences and aviation publications. Dorothy is the author and editor of a number of flying training books and has published articles in legal and insurance journals.

Daljeet Gill BA(Hons)

Daljeet is the Head of Design & Development for Pooleys Flight Equipment and editor of the Air Pilot's Manuals, Guides to the EASA IR & CPL Flight Test, Pre-flight Briefing and R/T Communications as well as many other publications. Daljeet has been involved with the editing, typesetting and designing of all Pooleys publications and products since she joined us in 2001. Graduating in 1999 with a BA(Hons) in Graphic Design, she deals with marketing, advertising, exhibition design and technical design of our manufactured products in the UK. She maintains our website and produces our Pooleys Catalogue. Daljeet's design skills and imaginative approach have brought a new level of clarity and readability to the projects she has touched.

Sebastian Pooley FRIN FRAeS

Sebastian is Managing Director of Pooleys Flight Equipment and a Director of Air Pilot Publishing. He holds a PPL (A). Sebastian is a Committee Member of the GANG - the General Aviation Navigation Group, part of the Royal Institute of Navigation and a judge for the International Dawn to Dusk Competition. He is a Liveryman of the Honourable Company of Air Pilots, a Fellow of the Royal Institute of Navigation and a Fellow of the Royal Aeronautical Society.

EASA PRIVATE PILOT LICENCE
AEROPLANE & HELICOPTER
COMMUNICATIONS

Before attempting these practice examination papers, you should have read Air Pilot's Manual, Volume 7 – Communications and have completed the Progress Tests throughout the manual.

The Communications examination consists of 12 questions; the time allowed is 20 minutes. Each of the practice examination papers that follow contain 20 questions.

The pass mark is 75%. You must get a minimum of 15 questions correct.

Please read each question carefully and ensure you understand it fully before making your choice of answer.

Each question is multiple choice with four possible answers A, B, C and D.

You should indicate your chosen answer by placing a cross in the appropriate box on the answer sheet.

Blank answer sheets are to be found at the end of this publication, these may be photocopied.

INTENTIONALLY BLANK

COMMUNICATIONS PAPER 1

1. The correct pronunciation for transmitting an altitude of 2500 is:

   a. Two fife zero zero

   b. Two fife hundred

   c. Too tousand fife hundred

   d. Too fife zero zero

2. The correct RTF phraseology for frequency 121.275 MHz is:

   a. One two one decimal two seven

   b. One two one two seven five

   c. One two one two seven

   d. One two one decimal two seven five

3. The word "Roger" has the meaning:

   a. I understand your last transmission

   b. Received and understood

   c. I will comply with your message

   d. I have received all of your last transmission

4. The transponder should be set to which code in the event of an emergency?

   a. 7000

   b. 7500

   c. 7600

   d. 7700

5. Readability 3 means:

   a. Perfectly readable

   b. Unreadable

   c. Readable but with difficulty

   d. Readable now and then

6. A service providing automated airfield and meteorological information for arriving and departing traffic is:

   a. AFIS

   b. ATIS

   c. FIS

   d. APIS

7. Distress is defined as a condition:

   a. Where the pilot considers the aircraft has an emergency

   b. Concerning the safety of an aircraft or other vehicle

   c. Of grave and/or imminent danger and of requiring immediate assistance

   d. Concerning the safety of an aircraft, or some person on board or within sight, and of not requiring immediate assistance

8. At what range on a straight in approach could you report "G-AJGV long final"?

   a. Between 8 nm and 4 nm

   b. Between 7 nm and 3 nm

   c. At 10 nm

   d. Between 9 nm and 5 nm

9. When requesting a MATZ transit, at what range/time (whichever is sooner) must the request be made?

    a. 20 nm or 10 minutes

    b. 15 nm or 5 minutes

    c. 10 nm or 10 minutes

    d. 15 nm or 10 minutes

10. LARS is an ATS surveillance service available to assist pilots flying outside controlled airspace. The service provided will be ..... or .....:

    a. Traffic service, Procedural service

    b. Procedural service, Deconfliction service

    c. Traffic service, Deconfliction service

    d. Basic service, Traffic service

11. The pressure setting 997 hectopascals is transmitted as:

    a. Pressure nine nine seven

    b. Nine nine seven

    c. Nine nine seven pressure setting

    d. Nine nine seven hectopascals

12. "STANDBY" means:

    a. The same as "pass your message"

    b. Wait and I will call you

    c. Repeat you last transmission

    d. Wait and transmit again

13. The instruction "SQUAWK IDENT" means:

    a. Operate the special position identification feature on the transponder

    b. Set the transponder to standby

    c. Set the transponder to ON

    d. Set the transponder to ALT

14. In the UK the three categories of Air Traffic Service are:

    a. Basic, Traffic and Deconfliction

    b. ATC, Flight Information Service, Air/Ground Communication Service

    c. Control, LARS, SVFR

    d. Radar, Tower, Procedural

15. On your initial call to an ATSU a pilot should pass:

    a. The aircraft call sign

    b. Aircraft call sign and type, departure and destination, position, and altitude

    c. The aircraft call sign, position and heading

    d. Aircraft call sign and service requested

16. Regarding VDF, a QDM is the:

    a. Magnetic bearing of the aircraft from the VDF station

    b. Magnetic heading (in nil wind) to steer to reach the VDF station

    c. True bearing of the aircraft from the VDF station

    d. True heading (in nil wind) to steer to reach the VDF station

17. The accuracy of a Class A VDF bearing is:

    a. $\pm 2°$

    b. $\pm 5°$

    c. $\pm 10°$

    d. $\pm 15°$

18.   A Special VFR clearance enables a pilot to:

   a.   Fly with lower weather minima

   b.   Cross an airway without needing a valid IR

   c.   Fly within a Control Zone in circumstances normally requiring an IFR clearance

   d.   Enter a Control Zone without clearance

19.   When using Safetycom, transmissions shall only be made within ....nm of the aerodrome of intended landing, and not above ...... feet AAL or ......feet above circuit height.

   a.   10 nm 3000 feet 1000 feet

   b.   10 nm 2000 feet 1000 feet

   c.   15 nm 2000 feet 1000 feet

   d.   15 nm 3000 feet 1000 feet

20.   121.5 MHz, the Aeronautical Emergency Frequency:

   a.   May be used to practise distress and urgency calls

   b.   May not be used to practise distress and urgency calls

   c.   May be used to practise distress but not urgency calls

   d.   May be used to practise urgency but not distress calls

---

END OF COMMUNICATIONS PAPER 1

No.	A	B	C	D
1			X	
2				X
3				X
4				X
5			X	
6		X		
7			X	
8	X			
9		X		
10			X	
11				X
12		X		
13	X			
14		X		
15				X
16		X		
17	X			
18			X	
19		X		
20				X

CORRECT ANSWERS: PERCENTAGES					
15	16	17	18	19	20
75%	80%	85%	90%	95%	100%

COMMUNICATIONS PAPER 1: EXPLANATIONS

Numeral or Numeral Element	Pronounciation
0	ZERO
1	WUN
2	TOO
3	TREE
4	FOW ER
5	FIFE
6	SIX
7	SEV EN
8	AIT
9	NIN ER
DECIMAL	DAYSEEMAL
HUNDRED	HUNDRED
THOUSAND	TOUSAND

1. **(Answer: C)** Altitude 2500 is pronounced **"too tousand fife hundred"**.

    When transmitting altitude, height, cloud height, visibility and runway visual range (basically anything measured in feet or metres!) whole hundreds and thousands are transmitted by stating the number of hundreds and thousands followed by the word "HUN-dred" or "TOU-SAND" as applicable. Combinations follow the same rule.

    FURTHER READING: APM VOLUME 7, SECTION 1, CHAPTER 2 – WHAT TO SAY

2. **(Answer: D)** The phraseology for 121.275 is "One two one decimal two seven five". If a number contains a decimal point the RTF word DAY-SEE-MAL is inserted at the appropriate point. When transmitting a frequency all six digits must be pronounced. The only exception being where the fifth and sixth number are both zeros, in which case only the first four digits will be pronounced, as in the first case below:

Number	Transmitted as:	Pronounced as:
121.100 MHz	One two one decimal one	Wun too wun dayseemal wun
120.925 MHz	One two zero decimal nine two five	Wun too zero dayseemal niner too fife
132.550 MHz	One three two decimal five five zero	Wun tree too dayseemal fife fife zero

    FURTHER READING: APM VOLUME 7, SECTION 1, CHAPTER 2 – WHAT TO SAY

3. **(Answer: D)** "Roger" has the meaning: I have received all of your last transmission. Note: Under no circumstances should this word be used in reply to a question requiring a direct answer in the affirmative (AFFIRM) or negative (NEGATIVE), or to acknowledge any item that must be readback.

    FURTHER READING: APM VOLUME 7, SECTION 1, CHAPTER 3 – AERODROME OPERATIONS

4. **(Answer: D)** An emergency is indicated by the transponder code 7700. The following special purpose codes are in use:

    7700: Emergency
    7600: Communications failure
    7500: Unlawful interference (hijack)
    7000: UK conspicuity code
    2000: Entering an FIR, from an adjacent region where the operation of transponders has not been required.

    FURTHER READING: APM VOLUME 7, SECTION 1, CHAPTER 1 – COCKPIT RADIOS

5. **(Answer: C)** Readability 3 means readable but with difficulty. *(See table right)*

    FURTHER READING: APM VOLUME 7, SECTION 1, CHAPTER 2 – WHAT TO SAY

Readability Scale	Meaning
1	Unreadable
2	Readable now and then
3	Readable but with difficulty
4	Readable
5	Perfectly readable

6. **(Answer: B)** ATIS, Automatic Terminal Information Service. At busier airports an Automatic Terminal Information Service is broadcast to provide a range of data, usually weather conditions and essential aerodrome information, on a discreet frequency or selected VOR.

    Each ATIS message is coded consecutively using the phonetic alphabet. A new message is generated at regular intervals (usually half hourly at the time of the routine meteorological observations at minutes 20 and 50) or whenever a significant change occurs.

    Pilots should advise ATC that they have received the latest ATIS:
    On Departure – before taxiing
    On Arrival – on first contact with the ATSU.

    FURTHER READING: APM VOLUME 7, SECTION 1, CHAPTER 4 – AERODROME INFORMATION

7. **(Answer: C)** DISTRESS is a condition of being threatened by grave and/or imminent danger, and of requiring immediate assistance. A distress message will take priority over all other messages.

    FURTHER READING: APM VOLUME 7, SECTION 3, CHAPTER 8 – EMERGENCY PROCEDURES

8. **(Answer: A)** "Long final" is between 8 nm and 4 nm.

    FURTHER READING: APM VOLUME 7, SECTION 1, CHAPTER 2 – WHAT TO SAY

9. **(Answer: B)** Civilian traffic wishing to penetrate a MATZ should make contact with the military controller 15 nm or 5 minutes flying time before reaching the zone boundary, whichever is sooner. On the initial call to the military controller the phrase "Request MATZ penetration" must be used, e.g. "Marham Zone, GMJDE request MATZ penetration".

    FURTHER READING: APM VOLUME 7, SECTION 1, CHAPTER 3 – AERODROME OPERATIONS

10. **(Answer: C)** Outside Controlled Airspace certain Air Traffic Service Units are able to provide a Lower Airspace Radar Service to pilots flying in UK uncontrolled airspace up to and including FL 95, within approximately 30 nm of each participating unit.

    FURTHER READING: APM VOLUME 7, SECTION 2, CHAPTER 6 – R/T IN UNCONTROLLED AIRSPACE

11. **(Answer: D)** The word "hectopascals" must be used when transmitting all pressure settings below 1000, e.g. QNH 994 hectopascals, QFE 987 hectopascals. This is to avoid any confusion with inches of mercury, the datum used in the United States.

    FURTHER READING: APM VOLUME 7, SECTION 1, CHAPTER 4 – AERODROME INFORMATION

12. **(Answer: B)** Standby means: wait and I will call you. ATC's response to your initial contact call will either be "pass your message" or "standby", the latter simply meaning that the controller is engaged with another task. You should say nothing in response to an instruction to "standby", simply wait and the controller will call you.

    FURTHER READING: APM VOLUME 7, SECTION 1, CHAPTER 2 – WHAT TO SAY

13. **(Answer: A)** "Squawk ident" means operate the special position identification feature on the transponder. The SPI feature is more usually referred to as the IDENT button. If a controller asks you to squawk "ident" you should press the ident button. This causes a flashing circle to appear around your aircraft's radar return confirming its identity to the controller.

Transponder phraseology:

PHRASE	MEANING
Squawk (code)	Set the code as instructed
Confirm Squawk	Confirm code set on the transponder
Reset (code)	Reselect assigned code
Squawk Ident	Operate the SPI feature
Squawk Mayday	Select emergency
Squawk Standby	Select the standby feature
Squawk Altitude	Select altitude reporting feature
Check altimeter setting and confirm (level)	Check pressure setting and report your level
Stop Squawk Altitude, wrong indication	Deselect pressure altitude reporting transmission as the indication is faulty
Stop Squawk Altitude	Deselect altitude reporting
Confirm (level)	Check and confirm your level. Used to verify the accuracy of the Mode C level information displayed to the controller

FURTHER READING: APM VOLUME 7, SECTION 1, CHAPTER 2 – WHAT TO SAY

14. **(Answer: B)** The UK has three main categories of aeronautical communication service: Air Traffic Control, Flight Information Service, Air/Ground Communication Service.

Air Traffic Control: A controller will issue instructions with which pilots must comply or, if the instruction is not suitable, the pilot must request an alternative clearance.

Flight Information Service: Provides information useful to the safe and efficient conduct of flights in the Aerodrome Traffic Zone. From this information pilots will be able to decide the appropriate course of action to be taken to ensure the safety of flight. Note: on the ground FISOs can issue instructions with which pilots should comply; in the air only information is passed.

Air/Ground: Only limited information is available and all decisions are the pilot's. The level of service is easily identifiable from the call sign used by the ground station.

UNIT	CALL SIGN	SERVICE
Area control centre	CONTROL	ATC
Radar (general)	RADAR	ATC
Approach control	APPROACH	ATC
Approach control radar arrivals	ARRIVAL/DIRECTOR	ATC
Approach control radar departures	DEPARTURE	ATC
Aerodrome control	TOWER	ATC
Surface movement control	GROUND	ATC
Flight information service	INFORMATION	FISO
Air/Ground Communication	RADIO	A/G

FURTHER READING: APM VOLUME 7, SECTION 1, CHAPTER 3 – AERODROME OPERATIONS

15. **(Answer: D)** The initial call to an ATS unit should only include the minimum information needed to establish:

   a)   the service that an en-route flight requires; or

   b)   the clearance/information that a joining or departing flight requires.

   The ATSU will then respond with "Pass Your Message" enabling more detailed information regarding the flight (ADDPAR) to be passed.

   FURTHER READING: APM VOLUME 7, SECTION 1, CHAPTER 3 – AERODROME OPERATIONS

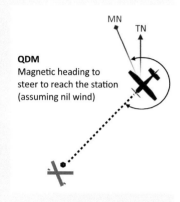

QDM
Magnetic heading to
steer to reach the station
(assuming nil wind)

16. **(Answer: B)** QDM is: The aircraft's magnetic heading to steer in zero wind to reach the station.

   ## OTHER VDF bearings available:

   QDR   AIRCRAFT'S MAGNETIC BEARING FROM THE STATION

   QTE   AIRCRAFT'S TRUE BEARING FROM THE STATION

   QUJ   AIRCRAFT'S TRUE TRACK TO THE STATION

   FURTHER READING: APM VOLUME 7, SECTION 2, CHAPTER 6 – R/T IN UNCONTROLLED AIRSPACE

17. **(Answer: A)** A Class A VDF bearing is accurate to +/- 2 degrees

   ACCURACY OF VDF Bearings:
   CLASS A +/- 2 degrees
   CLASS B +/- 5 degrees
   CLASS C +/- 10 degrees
   CLASS D accuracy less than class C

   FURTHER READING: APM VOLUME 7, SECTION 2, CHAPTER 6 – R/T IN UNCONTROLLED AIRSPACE

18. **(Answer: C)** A Special VFR clearance enables a pilot to fly within a Control Zone in circumstances normally requiring an IFR clearance. Special VFR clearances are only permitted within control ZONES, usually at the request of the pilot.

   Special VFR is a concession offered by ATC, which allows an aircraft to operate within a control zone which is Class A or in any other control zone in IMC, without requiring compliance with the Instrument Flight Rules. Instead pilots will comply with instructions given by the Air Traffic Control Unit.

   FURTHER READING: APM VOLUME 7, SECTION 2, CHAPTER 7 – R/T IN CONTROLLED AIRSPACE

19. **(Answer: B)** Safetycom is a common frequency introduced for use by aircraft in the vicinity of an airfield or landing site that does not have a notified VHF frequency for radio communications.

   The frequency is 135.475 MHz. Transmissions should only be made on Safetycom when aircraft are below 2000 ft above aerodrome/location elevation or below 1000 ft above promulgated circuit height. Transmissions shall also only be made within 10 nm of the aerodrome or intended landing site.

   FURTHER READING: APM VOLUME 7, SECTION 1, CHAPTER 3 – AERODROME OPERATIONS

20. **(Answer: D)** Pilots may simulate emergency incidents (BUT NOT THE STATE OF DISTRESS) on 121.5 MHz to enable them to gain experience of the ATC service available. Before calling, pilots should listen out on the emergency frequency to ensure that no actual or practice incident is already in progress. Simulated emergency calls must be prefixed PRACTICE and should be brief: "Practice Pan, Practice Pan, Practice Pan, London Centre G-BUGA". The emergency controller will then state whether the practice can be accepted.

FURTHER READING: APM VOLUME 7, SECTION 3, CHAPTER 8 – EMERGENCY PROCEDURES

END OF EXPLANATIONS PAPER 1

INTENTIONALLY BLANK

COMMUNICATIONS PAPER 2

1. The correct pronunciation for transmitting a height of 3400 is:

   a. Tree fower zero zero
   b. Tree tousand fower hundred
   c. Three thousand four hundred
   d. Three fower zero zero

2. The correct RTF phraseology for frequency 132.700 MHz is:

   a. One three two decimal seven
   b. One three two seven
   c. One three two point seven
   d. One three two decimal seven zero zero

3. The time 0734 is transmitted by radiotelephony as:

   a. Zero seven three four UTC
   b. Seven thirty four, or thirty four
   c. Zero seven three four, or three four
   d. Minute three four

4. You are asked by ATC "are you able to maintain VMC?" a correct reply would contain the phrase:

   a. Wilco
   b. Roger
   c. Affirm or negative
   d. Yes or no

5. The states of emergency are:

   a. Mayday and pan pan
   b. Difficulty and urgency
   c. Distress and urgency
   d. Mayday and distress

6. The correct abbreviation of the call sign "HELAIR GHBAH"

   a. Golf Alpha Hotel
   b. Helair Golf Alpha Hotel
   c. Bravo Alpha Hotel
   d. Helair Alpha Hotel

7. A distress call is preceded by the spoken word "MAYDAY", which is transmitted:

   a. Once
   b. Three times
   c. Twice
   d. Four times

8. Ideally, immediately following "mayday", an aircraft in distress should transmit:

   a. Call sign of the station addressed, time permitting
   b. Nature of the emergency
   c. The aircraft's call sign three times
   d. Altitude and present position

9. Pilots requesting a MATZ crossing should pass the following information when asked to do so by the military controller:

    a. Aircraft type, intention, departure and destination, route, POB
    b. A/c call sign, present position, next turning point, altitude
    c. A/c call sign, altitude, position, departure and destination, POB
    d. A/c call sign and type, departure point and destination, present position, altitude, request or intention

10. All messages relating to a climb or descent to a HEIGHT or ALTITUDE should:

    a. Use the word "TO" followed by the QFE or QNH
    b. Not use the word "TO"
    c. Use the word "TO" followed by the word HEIGHT or ALTITUDE
    d. Use the word "LEVEL" followed by the word HEIGHT or ALTITUDE

11. You make an initial call to an ATSU and in reply are told "G-MORG standby", you should:

    a. Say nothing and wait to be called
    b. Immediately say "standby G-MORG"
    c. Say "wilco"
    d. Call the ATSU again

12. The accuracy of a Class B VDF bearing is:

    a. ± 2°
    b. ± 5°
    c. ± 10°
    d. ± 15°

13. The Air Traffic Services available outside controlled airspace, are:

    a. Flight Information Service, Basic Service, Procedural Service and Traffic Service
    b. Basic Service, Traffic Information Service, Radar Information Service and Procedural Service
    c. Basic Service, Traffic Service, Deconfliction Service and Procedural Service
    d. Basic Service, Radar Traffic Service, Deconfliction Service and Radar Control Service

14. Which of the following is an example of a conditional clearance?

    a. G-AV behind the landing PA28 line up behind
    b. G-AV line up after the landing PA28
    c. G-AV take off at your discretion
    d. G-AV report final number 2

15. Conditional clearances are only used on an active runway when:

    a. It is very busy and it is CAVOK
    b. Aircraft wish to cross the active runway and it is safe
    c. The aircraft or vehicles concerned are visible to the controller and the pilot. The clearance relates to only one movement
    d. More than one aircraft is landing

16. In the first instance which frequency should be used for transmitting a MAYDAY?

    a. 121.5 MHz
    b. The civil or military frequency in use at the time
    c. The nearest MATZ
    d. Any local emergency frequency

17. The call sign pre-fix "STUDENT" indicates:

    a.   Training flights

    b.   A student pilot who is lost

    c.   A student pilot flying solo

    d.   A student pilot requiring extra assistance

18. An Air Traffic Service provided to give advice and information useful for the safe and efficient conduct of flight which may include weather information and general airspace activity, is:

    a.   Basic Service

    b.   Traffic Service

    c.   Deconfliction Service

    d.   Flight Information Service

19. "G-MOJE after departure cleared to zone boundary, via north lane, climb not above altitude 2,500 feet, squawk 4677". What type of message is this?

    a.   Take-off clearance

    b.   Route clearance

    c.   Conditional clearance

    d.   Airway joining clearance

20. You are making a standard overhead join, you have flown overhead at 2,000 feet AAL and are commencing your descent to circuit height. What RT call should you make?

    a.   "G-HE downwind descending"

    b.   "G-HE upwind descending"

    c.   "G-HE deadside descending"

    d.   "G-HE liveside descending"

END OF COMMUNICATIONS PAPER 2

	A	B	C	D
1.		X		
2.	X			
3.			X	
4.			X	
5.			X	
6.				X
7.		X		
8.	X			
9.				X
10.			X	
11.	X			
12.		X		
13.			X	
14.	X			
15			X	
16.		X		
17.			X	
18.	X			
19.		X		
20.			X	

CORRECT ANSWERS: PERCENTAGES					
15	16	17	18	19	20
75%	80%	85%	90%	95%	100%

COMMUNICATIONS PAPER 2: EXPLANATIONS

Numeral or Numeral Element	Pronounciation
0	ZERO
1	WUN
2	TOO
3	TREE
4	FOW ER
5	FIFE
6	SIX
7	SEV EN
8	AIT
9	NIN ER
DECIMAL	DAYSEEMAL
HUNDRED	HUNDRED
THOUSAND	TOUSAND

1. **(Answer: B)** Note in this question you are asked for the pronunciation. Height 3400 is pronounced "tree tousand fower hundred".

   When transmitting altitude, height, cloud height, visibility and runway visual range (basically anything measured in feet or metres!)whole hundreds and thousands are transmitted by stating the number of hundreds and thousands followed by the word "HUN-dred" or "TOU-SAND" as applicable. Combinations follow the same rule.

   FURTHER READING: APM VOLUME 7, SECTION 1, CHAPTER 2 – WHAT TO SAY

2. **(Answer: A)** The phraseology for 132.700 is "One three two decimal seven". If a number contains a decimal point the RTF word DAY-SEE-MAL is inserted at the appropriate point. When transmitting a frequency all six digits must be pronounced. The only exception being where the fifth and sixth number are both zeros, in which case only the first four digits will be pronounced:

Frequency	Transmitted as:	No. of digits to be transmitted
Fifth and sixth digits **BOTH ZERO**		
121.0**00** 132.7**00**	ONE TWO ONE DECIMAL ZERO ONE THREE TWO DECIMAL SEVEN	4
All six numbers pronounced		
119.055 122.405 133.075 135.725	ONE ONE NINE DECIMAL ZERO FIVE FIVE ONE TWO TWO DECIMAL FOUR ZERO FIVE ONE THREE THREE DECIMAL ZERO SEVEN FIVE ONE THREE FIVE DECIMAL SEVEN TWO FIVE	6
Only the last digit is zero, so all six numbers must be pronounced		
118.050 126.450 131.650	ONE ONE EIGHT DECIMAL ZERO FIVE ZERO ONE TWO SIX DECIMAL FOUR FIVE ZERO ONE THREE ONE DECIMAL SIX FIVE ZERO	6

   FURTHER READING: APM VOLUME 7, SECTION 1, CHAPTER 2 – WHAT TO SAY

3. **(Answer: C)** Co-ordinated Universal Time (UTC) is to be used at all times; UTC is also known as Zulu and is the same as GMT. Normally when transmitting time only the minutes of the hour are required. If there is a possibility of confusion the hour should be included as well.

Time	Transmitted as:	Pronounced as:
0805	ZERO FIVE (or zero eight zero five)	ZERO FIFE
1300	ONE THREE ZERO ZERO	WUN TREE ZERO ZERO
2258	FIVE EIGHT (or two two five eight)	FIFE AIT

   FURTHER READING: APM VOLUME 7, SECTION 1, CHAPTER 2 – WHAT TO SAY

4. **(Answer: C)** In response to a direct question use "affirm" or "negative" as appropriate. "Roger" only means: I have received all of your last transmission. It does not answer the question!

   FURTHER READING: APM VOLUME 7, SECTION 1, CHAPTER 2 – WHAT TO SAY

5. **(Answer: C)** Distress and urgency are two states of emergency. They are defined as:

    DISTRESS is a condition of being threatened by grave and/or imminent danger and of requiring immediate assistance. A distress message will take priority over all other messages.

    URGENCY is a condition concerning the safety of an aircraft or other vehicle, or of some other person on board or within sight, but not requiring immediate assistance.

    FURTHER READING: APM VOLUME 7, SECTION 3, CHAPTER 8 – EMERGENCY PROCEDURES

6. **(Answer: D)** The abbreviation of Helair G-HBAH is "Helair Alpha Hotel". Call sign abbreviations follow three patterns:

Full Call Sign		Abbreviated Call Sign
G-AJGV Piper G-MACK* Citation G-HBAH*	**AIRCRAFT REGISTRATION:** The first and the last two characters of the aircraft registration	G-GV Piper CK Citation AH
Either the manufacturer's name or the name of aircraft model may be used to prefix the call sign in place of the first character		
Modernair G-BNPL Britannia G-MORG	The telephony designator of the aircraft operating agency, followed by the last two characters of the registration marking of the aircraft.	Modernair PL Britannia RG
Modernair 012 Monarch 416	**Flight Number:** No abbreviation permitted.	Modernair 012 Monarch 416

FURTHER READING: APM VOLUME 7, SECTION 1, CHAPTER 3 – AERODROME OPERATIONS

7. **(Answer: B)** A distress call begins with the word "MAYDAY" spoken three times.

    FURTHER READING: APM VOLUME 7, SECTION 3, CHAPTER 8 – EMERGENCY PROCEDURES

8. **(Answer: A)** Immediately after "Mayday" the pilot of an aircraft in distress should ideally transmit the call sign of the station being addressed. A distress call begins with the word "MAYDAY" spoken three times; the subsequent information should then be passed ideally in the order below:

MAYDAY MAYDAY MAYDAY	
C	Call sign of station addressed
A	Aircraft call sign
T	Type
N	Nature of the emergency
I	Intentions of pilot-in-command
P	Present (or last known) position; altitude/flight level; heading
P	Pilot qualifications, eg. student pilot; PPL; IMC; IR
O	Other useful information, eg. number on board, fuel endurance

FURTHER READING: APM VOLUME 7, SECTION 3, CHAPTER 8 – EMERGENCY PROCEDURES

9. **(Answer: D)** When instructed by an ATS Unit to "Pass your message", your reply should contain the following information, ideally in the order specified. ADDPAR is a mnemonic that may be used to keep the details in the correct order:

A	Aircraft call sign and type
D	Departure point
D	Destination
P	Present Position
A	Altitude/Level
R	Request, intentions or additional details (eg. flight rules, next route point, request–whatever is applicable to the flight)

This call format is appropriate for giving your flight details in many situations including rejoin, obtaining a radar service or basic service, requesting transit of a MATZ or permission to enter a Control Zone.

FURTHER READING: APM VOLUME 7, SECTION 1, CHAPTER 3 – AERODROME OPERATIONS

10. **(Answer: C)** In communications relating to a climb or descent to a height or altitude the word "TO" is used. The word "TO" is to be omitted when referring to Flight Levels. For example:

Golf-Alpha Victor request climb flight level three five

As opposed to:

Golf-Alpha Victor request climb TO altitude three thousand five hundred feet

FURTHER READING: APM VOLUME 7, SECTION 2, CHAPTER 6 – R/T IN UNCONTROLLED AIRSPACE

11. **(Answer: A)** Standby means: wait and I will call you. ATC's response your initial contact call will either be "pass your message" or "standby", the latter simply meaning that the controller is engaged with another task. You should say nothing in response to an instruction to "standby", simply wait and the controller will call you.

FURTHER READING: APM VOLUME 7, SECTION 1, CHAPTER 2 – WHAT TO SAY

12. **(Answer: B)** A Class B VDF bearing is accurate to +/- 5 degrees

ACCURACY OF VDF Bearings:
CLASS A +/- 2 degrees
CLASS B +/- 5 degrees
CLASS C +/- 10 degrees
CLASS D accuracy less than class C

FURTHER READING: APM VOLUME 7, SECTION 2, CHAPTER 6 – R/T IN UNCONTROLLED AIRSPACE

13. **(Answer: C)** The Air Traffic Services available outside controlled airspace are Basic Service, Traffic Service, Deconfliction Service and Procedural Service.

FURTHER READING: APM VOLUME 7, SECTION 2, CHAPTER 6 – R/T IN UNCONTROLLED AIRSPACE

14. **(Answer: A)** It is a Conditional Clearance which may be issued to help the traffic flow. This will relate to one movement only, and if the subject aircraft is landing it must be the next to land. It is vital that the pilot has identified the subject aircraft correctly. If there is any doubt - ask!

    The format or a conditional clearance will be:
    - *Call sign*
    - *The condition*
    - *Identification of the subject of the condition*
    - *Reiteration of the condition*

    FURTHER READING: APM VOLUME 7, SECTION 1, CHAPTER 3 – AERODROME OPERATIONS

15. **(Answer: C)** Conditional clearances will not be used for movements affecting the active runway, except when the aircraft or vehicles concerned are visible to both the controller and pilot. Conditional clearances will relate to one movement only and, in the case of landing traffic, this must be the first aircraft on approach.

    FURTHER READING: APM VOLUME 7, SECTION 1, CHAPTER 3 – AERODROME OPERATIONS

16. **(Answer: B)** The first attempt to transmit an emergency message should be made on the frequency currently in use. If this is not successful the pilot should transmit his/her intention is to change to the Aeronautical Emergency Frequency 121.5 MHz.

    FURTHER READING: APM VOLUME 7, SECTION 3, CHAPTER 8– EMERGENCY PROCEDURES

17. **(Answer: C)** On initial contact, student pilots who are flying solo shall use the call sign prefix 'STUDENT'. Once acknowledged, it is not normally necessary for student pilots to use the prefix in subsequent transmissions, unless they feel they are being asked to do something with which they are not familiar.

    FURTHER READING: APM VOLUME 7, SECTION 1, CHAPTER 3 – AERODROME OPERATIONS

18. **(Answer: A)** The Basic Service is an Air Traffic Service provided to give advice and information useful to the safe and efficient conduct of flights. Such items may include weather information, changes in the serviceability of facilities, conditions at aerodromes or general aerial activity information.
    - *The service is available to IFR or VFR flights, but may not be appropriate for flight in IMC.*
    - *Traffic Information should not be expected. Outside an ATZ there is no obligation for the controller/FISO to pass Traffic Information.*

    FURTHER READING: APM VOLUME 7, SECTION 2, CHAPTER 6 – R/T IN UNCONTROLLED AIRSPACE

19. **(Answer: B)** "G-MOJE after departure cleared to zone boundary, via north lane, climb not above altitude 2,500 feet, squawk 4677". This is a route clearance.

Contents of a Clearance
- Aircraft Identification
- Clearance Limit
- Route
- Level of Flight

The following may be included:
- Communication Instructions
- Any Special Instructions eg. SSR, Approach or Departure Manoeuvres

FURTHER READING: APM VOLUME 7, SECTION 2, CHAPTER 7 – R/T IN UNCONTROLLED AIRSPACE

20. **(Answer: C)** The standard overhead join is a procedure often used at smaller aerodromes. The aircraft is required to:
   a. Overfly the aerodrome at 2000 feet above aerodrome elevation
   b. Determine the circuit direction if not already known (signal square, windsock, other traffic)
   c. Descend on the "dead side" to circuit height:
   d. Join the circuit by crossing the upwind end of the runway at circuit height.
   e. Position downwind

FURTHER READING: APM VOLUME 7, SECTION 1, CHAPTER 3 – AERODROME OPERATIONS

END OF EXPLANATIONS PAPER 2

INTENTIONALLY BLANK

1. The correct pronunciation for transmitting an altitude of 14,500, is:

   a.   Wun fower thousand five zero zero

   b.   Fourteen thousand fife hundred

   c.   Wun fower tousand fife hundred

   d.   One four tousand five hundred

2. The correct pronunciation for the frequency 129.400 Mhz, is:

   a.   One two nine decimal four

   b.   Wun too niner dayseemal fower

   c.   Wun too niner point four

   d.   One two nine decimal four zero zero

3. The time 1130 is pronounced as:

   a.   Eleven thirty

   b.   Wun wun tree zero, or tree zero

   c.   One one three zero, or three zero

   d.   Half past eleven

4. The transponder should be set to which code in the event of a radio failure?

   a.   7700

   b.   7600

   c.   7500

   d.   7400

5. Readability 4 means:

   a.   Perfectly readable

   b.   Unreadable

   c.   Readable

   d.   Readable now and then

6. What does "ATIS" stand for?

   a.   Aeronautical Traffic Information Service

   b.   Automatic Terminal Information Service

   c.   Air Traffic Information Service

   d.   Airport Terminal Information Service

7. Urgency is defined as a condition:

   a.   Where the pilot considers the aircraft has an emergency

   b.   Concerning the safety of another aircraft or other vehicle requiring immediate assistance

   c.   Of grave and/or imminent danger and of requiring immediate assistance

   d.   Concerning the safety of an aircraft or other vehicle, or some person on board or within sight, and not requiring immediate assistance

8. The correct radio call to make when you are ready for take-off is:

   a.   Request take- off

   b.   Ready for take-off

   c.   Ready

   d.   Ready for departure

9. If you are cleared to a HEIGHT of 2500 feet, what pressure setting should be used?

   a.   QNE

   b.   QNH

   c.   QFF

   d.   QFE

10. Following the MAYDAY prefix and the call sign of the station addressed, the correct sequence for the subsequent content of a distress message, is:

    a. Aircraft call sign, type, the nature of the emergency and position

    b. Aircraft call sign, type, the nature of the emergency and intention of the commander

    c. Position, POB, Aircraft call sign, type, and the nature of the emergency

    d. Aircraft call sign, type, nature of the emergency and POB

11. You are en route receiving a service from a radar unit, you are asked "G-AJGV Confirm your level", the purpose of this is to:

    a. Check the altimeter setting you are using

    b. Check that altitude reporting is selected

    c. Verify the accuracy of the altitude information displayed to the controller

    d. Check your position

12. The correct phraseology format to use when requesting a true bearing, is:

    a. True bearing true bearing, G-MORG request true bearing G-MORG

    b. Request QTE G-MORG

    c. G-MORG request true bearing

    d. G-MORG request QTE G-MORG

13. The correct format for a conditional clearance, is:

    a. Call sign, condition, instruction, identification of the subject of the condition

    b. Call sign, identification of the subject of the condition, condition, instruction

    c. Call sign, instruction, identification of the subject of the condition, condition

    d. Call sign, condition, identification of the subject of the condition, reiteration of the condition

14. A Procedural Service is an Air Traffic Service in which:

    a. Basic Service is not provided, but safety critical information is provided

    b. In addition to a Basic Service, aircraft participating in the service will be deconflicted as long as the pilots comply with ATC instructions

    c. In addition to a Basic Service the controller provides specific surveillance derived traffic information

    d. Basic Service is not provided, but aircraft participating in the service will be deconflicted as long as the pilots comply with instructions

15. "G-MJDE after departure cleared to zone boundary, via north lane, climb not above altitude 2,500 feet, squawk 4677". In relation to this message what is the clearance limit?

    a. 2,500 feet

    b. The north lane

    c. The zone boundary

    d. There is no clearance limit stated

16. After establishing two way communication and being asked to "pass your message", pilots requiring ATSOCAS should pass:

    a. A/c call sign, present position, next turning point, altitude

    b. A/c call sign and type, departure point and destination, present position, altitude, request or intention

    c. Aircraft type, intention, departure and destination, route, POB

    d. A/c call sign, altitude, position, departure and destination, POB

17. On hearing a distress message a pilot should:

    a. Immediately attempt to relay

    b. Maintain radio silence

    c. Change frequency

    d. Request a frequency change from ATC

18. You are receiving a Traffic Service and have been asked to report your heading. You have done so twice, and then hear: "G-HH reply not received if you read Thames Radar turn left heading 120 degrees, I say again turn left heading 120 degrees". What may have occurred:

    a.   You have a receiver failure

    b.   You are out of range

    c.   The controller has not been paying attention

    d.   You have a transmitter failure

19. Which of the following groups must be read back in full?

    a.   All messages from ATC and FIS, but not from Air/Ground

    b.   Level instructions, Headings, VDF information and surface wind

    c.   Clearance to land on or enter an active runway, transponder codes, VDF.

    d.   Frequency changes, pressure settings and visibility

20. A Special VFR clearance enables a pilot to:

    a.   Fly with lower weather minima

    b.   Cross an airway without needing a valid IR

    c.   Fly within a Control Zone in circumstances normally requiring an IFR clearance

    d.   Enter a Control Zone without clearance

END OF COMMUNICATIONS PAPER 3

COMMUNICATIONS PAPER 3: ANSWERS

	A	B	C	D
1.			X	
2.		X		
3.		X		
4.		X		
5.			X	
6.		X		
7.				X
8.				X
9.				X
10.		X		
11.			X	
12.	X			
13.				X
14.		X		
15			X	
16.		X		
17.		X		
18.				X
19.			X	
20.			X	

CORRECT ANSWERS: PERCENTAGES					
15	16	17	18	19	20
75%	80%	85%	90%	95%	100%

COMMUNICATIONS PAPER 3: EXPLANATIONS

Numeral or Numeral Element	Pronounciation
0	ZERO
1	WUN
2	TOO
3	TREE
4	FOW ER
5	FIFE
6	SIX
7	SEV EN
8	AIT
9	NIN ER
DECIMAL	DAYSEEMAL
HUNDRED	HUNDRED
THOUSAND	TOUSAND

1. **(Answer: C)** Altitude 14,500 is pronounced "wun fower tousand fife hundred". When transmitting altitude, height, cloud height, visibility and runway visual range (basically anything measured in feet or metres!) whole hundreds and thousands are transmitted by stating the number of hundreds and thousands followed by the word "HUN-dred" or "TOU-SAND" as applicable. Combinations follow the same rule.

FURTHER READING: APM VOLUME 7, SECTION 1, CHAPTER 2 – WHAT TO SAY

2. **(Answer: B)** You are asked for the pronunciation for 129.400. It is "Wun too niner dayseemal fower". If a number contains a decimal point the RTF word DAY-SEE-MAL is inserted at the appropriate point. When transmitting a frequency all six digits must be pronounced. The only exception being where the fifth and sixth number are both zeros, in which case only the first four digits will be pronounced.

Number	Transmitted as:	Pronounced as:
121.100 MHz	One two one decimal one	Wun too wun dayseemal wun
120.925 MHz	One two zero decimal nine two five	Wun too zero dayseemal niner too fife
132.550 MHz	One three two decimal five five zero	Wun tree too dayseemal fife fife zero

FURTHER READING: APM VOLUME 7, SECTION 1, CHAPTER 2 – WHAT TO SAY

3. **(Answer: B)** Note you are asked for the pronunciation, 1130 is spoken as "wun wun tree zero" or "tree zero". Normally when transmitting time only the minutes of the hour are required. If there is a possibility of confusion the hour should be included as well.

Time	Transmitted as:	Pronounced as:
0805	ZERO FIVE (or zero eight zero five)	ZERO FIFE
1300	ONE THREE ZERO ZERO	WUN TREE ZERO ZERO
2258	FIVE EIGHT (or two two five eight)	FIFE AIT

FURTHER READING: APM VOLUME 7, SECTION 1, CHAPTER 2 – WHAT TO SAY

4. **(Answer: B)** Radio failure is indicated by the transponder code 7600. The following special purpose codes are in use:

- **7700:** Emergency
- **7600:** Communications failure
- **7500:** Unlawful interference (hijack)
- **7000:** UK conspicuity code
- **2000:** Entering an FIR, from an adjacent region where the operation of transponders has not been required

FURTHER READING: APM VOLUME 7, SECTION 1, CHAPTER 1 – COCKPIT RADIOS

5. **(Answer: C)** Readability 4 means "readable".

FURTHER READING: APM VOLUME 7, SECTION 1, CHAPTER 3 – AERODROME OPERATIONS

Readability Scale	Meaning
1	Unreadable
2	Readable now and then
3	Readable but with difficulty
4	Readable
5	Perfectly readable

6. **(Answer: B)** ATIS, Automatic Terminal Information Service. At busier airports an Automatic Terminal Information Service is broadcast to provide a range of data, usually weather conditions and essential aerodrome information, on a discreet frequency or selected VOR. Each ATIS message is coded consecutively using the phonetic alphabet. A new message is generated at regular intervals (usually half hourly at the time of the routine meteorological observations at minutes 20 and 50) or whenever a significant change occurs. Pilots should advise ATC that they have received the latest ATIS:

On Departure – before taxiing

On Arrival – on first contact with the ATSU.

FURTHER READING: APM VOLUME 7, SECTION 1, CHAPTER 4 – AERODROME INFORMATION

7. **(Answer: D)** Urgency is a condition concerning the safety of an aircraft or other vehicle, or of some other person on board or within sight, but not requiring immediate assistance.

FURTHER READING: APM VOLUME 7, SECTION 3, CHAPTER 8 – EMERGENCY PROCEDURES

8. **(Answer: D)** So that no misunderstanding arises, unless an aircraft is actually being "Cleared for Takeoff", the word "Departure" is to be used by both controllers and pilots.

FURTHER READING: APM VOLUME 7, SECTION 1, CHAPTER 2 – WHAT TO SAY

9. **(Answer: D)** Height is defined as the vertical distance of a level, point or object considered as a point measured from a specified datum. The datum is normally the highest point on the landing area. With QFE set the aircraft altimeter will indicate height above the aerodrome. The phraseology used when referring to vertical position differs depending on the pressure setting in use:

If QFE is set:	"Height (number) feet"
If QNH is set:	"Altitude (number) feet"
If standard 1013 hPa is set (SPS):	"Flight level (number)"

FURTHER READING: APM VOLUME 7, SECTION 1, CHAPTER 4 – AERODROME INFORMATION

10. **(Answer: B)** The format for a distress call is:

MAYDAY MAYDAY MAYDAY	
C	Call sign of station addressed
A	Aircraft call sign
T	Type
N	Nature of the emergency
I	Intentions of pilot-in-command
P	Present (or last known) position; altitude/flight level; heading
P	Pilot qualifications, eg. student pilot; PPL; IMC; IR
O	Other useful information, eg. number on board, fuel endurance

FURTHER READING: APM VOLUME 7, SECTION 3, CHAPTER 8 – EMERGENCY PROCEDURES

11. **(Answer: C)** "Confirm your level" is used to verify the accuracy of the level information displayed to the controller.

Transponder Phraseology:	
PHRASE	**MEANING**
Squawk (code)	Set the code as instructed
Confirm Squawk	Confirm code set on the transponder
Reset (code)	Reselect assignment code
Squawk Ident	Operate the SPI feature
Squawk Mayday	Select emergency
Squawk Standby	Select the standby feature
Squawk Altitude	Select altitude reporting feature
Check altimeter setting and confirm (level)	Check pressure setting and report your level
Stop Squawk Altitude, wrong indication	Deselect pressure altitude reporting transmission as the indication is faulty
Stop Squawk Altitude	Deselect altitude reporting
Confirm (level)	Check and confirm your level. Used to verify the accuracy of the Mode C level information displayed to the controller

FURTHER READING: APM VOLUME 7, SECTION 1, CHAPTER 1 – COCKPIT RADIOS

12. **(Answer: A)** The correct RTF phraseology format to use when requesting a true bearing, is: "True bearing true bearing, G-MORG request true bearing G-MORG". Notice that this phraseology is different from that used when requesting other bearing information, which should follow the format: (Full call sign) request QDM/QDR (Full call sign)

FURTHER READING: APM VOLUME 7, SECTION 2, CHAPTER 6 – R/T IN UNCONTROLLED AIRSPACE

13. **(Answer: D)** The format for a conditional clearance will be:

- Call sign
- The condition
- Identification of the subject of the condition
- Reiteration of the condition

For example: "G-HHAV hold position BEHIND the landing Boeing 737 line up and wait runway 26 behind"

FURTHER READING: APM VOLUME 7, SECTION 1, CHAPTER 3 – AERODROME OPERATIONS

14. **(Answer: B)** A Procedural Service is an ATS where, in addition to the provision of a Basic Service, the controller provides vertical, lateral, longitudinal and time instructions, which if complied with will achieve the deconfliction minima against other aircraft participating in the Procedural Service.

A Procedural Service is most commonly found at ATC Units without surveillance radar equipment at airfields with notified instrument procedures for approach, holding and departure. Pilots flying in the vicinity of aerodromes having instrument approaches outside controlled airspace are encouraged to establish RTF contact with the appropriate ATC Unit.

Since the service does not involve radar derived information, and as traffic does not legally need to be in contact with a procedural unit in Class F and G airspace, you should be aware that there is a high likelihood of encountering conflicting traffic without any warnings from ATC.

FURTHER READING: APM VOLUME 7, SECTION 2, CHAPTER 6 – R/T IN UNCONTROLLED AIRSPACE

15. **(Answer: C)** Clearance Limit: The point to which an aircraft is granted an Air Traffic Control clearance. In this case the clearance limit is the zone boundary.

A clearance may vary in complexity from a detailed description of the route and levels to be flown (at busier airports condensed to standard instrument departures) to a brief landing clearance. Clearances are required for any flight, or portion of flight for which an Air Traffic Control or an Air Traffic advisory service is provided.

FURTHER READING: APM VOLUME 7, SECTION 1, CHAPTER 3 – AERODROME OPERATIONS

---

16. **(Answer: B)** When instructed by an ATS Unit to "Pass your message", your reply should contain the following information, ideally in the order specified. ADDPAR is a mnemonic that may be used to keep the details in the correct order:

A	Aircraft call sign and type
D	Departure point
D	Destination
P	Present Position
A	Altitude/Level
R	Request, intentions or additional details (eg. flight rules, next route point, request–whatever is applicable to the flight)

FURTHER READING: APM VOLUME 7, SECTION 1, CHAPTER 3 – AERODROME OPERATIONS

---

17. **(Answer: B)** Transmissions from aircraft in distress have priority over all other transmissions. On hearing a distress call, all stations must maintain radio silence on that frequency unless:

- The distress is cancelled or the distress traffic is terminated;
- The distress traffic has been transferred to another frequency;
- The station controlling communications gives permission; or
- The station itself has to render assistance.

FURTHER READING: APM VOLUME 7, SECTION 3, CHAPTER 8 – EMERGENCY PROCEDURES

---

18. **(Answer: D)** You have a transmitter failure. By asking you to turn, the controller is trying to establish whether you are still able to receive messages (the transponder ident feature may also be used for this purpose). If you did receive and comply with the instruction you would probably hear something like:

"G-HH turn observed I will continue to pass instructions".

FURTHER READING: APM VOLUME 7, SECTION 3, CHAPTER 9– RADIO FAILURE PROCEDURES

---

19. **(Answer: C)** Read back requirements were introduced in the interests of flight safety to ensure that the message has been received correctly as intended. The stringency of the requirement to readback is directly related to the possible seriousness of a misunderstanding. Reading back also ensures that the correct aircraft and that aircraft alone will act upon the instruction given. The ATC messages listed in the table below must be read back in full. If a pilot fails to read back any of these items the controller will ask him/her to do so.

- **Level instructions**
- **Heading instructions**
- **Speed instructions**
- **Airways or route clearances**
- **Approach clearances**
- **Runway in use**
- **Clearances to enter, land on, take off from, backtrack, cross or hold short of an active runway**
- **SSR (transponder) operating instructions**
- **Altimeter settings**
- **VDF information**
- **Frequency changes**
- **Type of radar service**
- **Taxi instructions**
- **Transition levels**

FURTHER READING: APM VOLUME 7, SECTION 1, CHAPTER 3 – AERODROME OPERATIONS

20. **(Answer: C)** A Special VFR clearance enables a pilot to fly within a Control Zone in circumstances normally requiring an IFR clearance. Special VFR clearances are only permitted within Control ZONES, usually at the request of the pilot. Special VFR is a concession offered by ATC, which allows an aircraft to operate within a control zone which is Class A or in any other control zone in IMC, without requiring compliance with the Instrument Flight Rules. Instead they will comply with instructions given by the Air Traffic Control Unit.

FURTHER READING: APM VOLUME 7, SECTION 2, CHAPTER 7 – R/T IN CONTROLLED AIRSPACE

END OF EXPLANATIONS PAPER 3

INTENTIONALLY BLANK

COMMUNICATIONS PAPER 4

1. The time 2150 is transmitted by radiotelephony as:

   a. Two one five zero, or five zero

   b. Twenty one fifty

   c. Two one fifty

   d. Ten to ten

2. A distress call must be preceded by the prefix:

   a. PAN PAN or MAYDAY transmitted twice

   b. MAYDAY transmitted once

   c. MAYDAY transmitted three times

   d. PAN PAN transmitted three times

3. LARS is an ATS surveillance service available to assist pilots flying outside controlled airspace. The service provided will be ..... or .....:

   a. Traffic service, Procedural service

   b. Procedural service, Deconfliction service

   c. Traffic service, Deconfliction service

   d. Basic service, Traffic service

4. When may the phrase "take-off" be used by a pilot?

   a. Only when ready for departure

   b. Only when acknowledging take-off clearance

   c. Only ATC may use this phrase

   d. Only when the power checks are complete

5. Within UK airspace when clearing an aircraft to a HEIGHT a controller will include the:

   a. QNH

   b. Regional pressure setting

   c. QFE

   d. Standard pressure setting

6. Aeronautical messages are prioritised. Which of the following is true?

   a. Flight safety messages are handled before Urgency messages

   b. Flight regularity messages are handled before VDF messages

   c. VDF messages are handled before flight safety messages

   d. Meteorological messages are handled before VDF messages

7. A Flight Information Service at an aerodrome provides:

   a. Instructions to aircraft within the ATZ

   b. Information to aircraft within the ATZ

   c. Information to aircraft within 15 nm of the aerodrome

   d. Control of aircraft in the ATZ

8. The correct phraseology format to use when requesting a QDM is:

   a. QDM,QDM, QDM, G-MACK request QDM

   b. Request QDM G-MACK

   c. G-MACK request QDM

   d. G-MACK request QDM G-MACK

9. An Air Traffic Service where a controller passes specific surveillance derived traffic information, but the avoidance of other traffic is the pilot's responsibility, is:

    a. Basic Service

    b. Traffic Service

    c. Deconfliction Service

    d. Procedural Service

10. After establishing two-way communication and being asked to "pass your message", pilots requiring a LARS should pass:

    a. A/c call sign, altitude, position, departure and destination, POB

    b. Aircraft type, intention, departure and destination, route, POB

    c. A/c call sign and type, departure point and destination, present position, altitude, request or intention

    d. A/c call sign, present position, next turning point, altitude

11. Which of the following statements is true regarding the characteristics of VHF propagation?

    a. The VHF band extends from 3 to 30 MHz and the range is limited by line of sight

    b. The VHF band extends from 30 to 300 MHz and the range is limited by line of sight

    c. The VHF band uses sky waves to achieve ranges of up to 1200 nm

    d. VHF is only used for voice communications and the VHF band extends from 30 to 300 KHz

12. When wanting to transit a MATZ a pilot must establish two way communication with the aerodrome controlling the zone by ...(i)..., or ...(ii)... from the boundary whichever is the sooner:

    a. i) 10 nm   ii) 5 minutes

    b. i) 10 nm   ii) 10 minutes

    c. i) 15 nm   ii) 5 minutes

    d. i) 15 nm   ii) 10 minutes

13. How should a pilot in an emergency transmit the aircraft's position?

    a. Present (or last known) position; altitude/flight level; heading

    b. In relation to the nearest VOR/DME

    c. Present (or last known) Position

    d. The last position passed by radar

14. In the Pooley's Flight Guide you read that ALBAN, your intended destination, has an Air/Ground Communication Service. When addressing ALBAN what call sign should you use?

    a. ALBAN APPROACH

    b. ALBAN INFORMATION

    c. ALBAN RADIO

    d. ALBAN GROUND

15. Regarding VDF, a QDR is the:

    a. Magnetic bearing of the aircraft from the VDF station

    b. Magnetic heading (in nil wind) to steer to reach the VDF station

    c. True bearing of the aircraft from the VDF station

    d. True heading (in nil wind) to steer to reach the VDF station

16. In circumstances where a pilot is responsible for activating a flight plan, this may be achieved by:

    a. Requesting that the flight plan be activated on a FIS frequency, avoiding busy frequencies

    b. Using the radio to ask an ATSU to activate the plan

    c. Telephone prior to departure, and must not be done in flight

    d. Requesting permission to enter controlled airspace, only when within controlled airspace can the plan be activated.

17. You are arriving at an airfield, the FISO is using the call sign suffix "INFORMATION" and tells you: "G-BH, Land at your discretion, surface wind 300/8"

    a. My discretion, surface wind 300/8 G-BH

    b. Roger G-BH

    c. Cleared to land G-BH

    d. Land at my discretion G-BH

18. A QNH of 981 hectopascals is transmitted as:

    a. QNH nine eight one

    b. Pressure nine eight one

    c. QNH nine eight one hectopascals

    d. Nine eight one

19. What is VOLMET?

    a. Meteorological reports for an individual airport broadcast on a discrete frequency or VOR

    b. Meteorological reports and airfield information for an individual airport broadcast on a discrete frequency or VOR

    c. Meteorological reports identified by a code letter broadcast on a discrete frequency

    d. Meteorological reports for certain groups of airfields broadcast on specified frequencies

20. When reading back an ATC instruction, you should end the message with:

    a. Your aircraft call sign

    b. The ground station call sign

    c. "Over"

    d. "Out"

END OF COMMUNICATIONS PAPER 4

No.	A	B	C	D
1	X			
2			X	
3			X	
4		X		
5			X	
6			X	
7		X		
8				X
9		X		
10			X	
11		X		
12			X	
13	X			
14			X	
15	X			
16		X		
17		X		
18			X	
19				X
20	X			

CORRECT ANSWERS: PERCENTAGES					
15	16	17	18	19	20
75%	80%	85%	90%	95%	100%

1. **(Answer: A)** Co-ordinated Universal Time (UTC) is to be used at all times; UTC is also known as Zulu and is the same as GMT. Normally when transmitting time only the minutes of the hour are required. If there is a possibility of confusion the hour should be included as well.

Time	Transmitted as:	Pronounced as:
0805	ZERO FIVE (or zero eight zero five)	ZERO FIFE
1300	ONE THREE ZERO ZERO	WUN TREE ZERO ZERO
2258	FIVE EIGHT (or two two five eight)	FIFE AIT

FURTHER READING: APM VOLUME 7, SECTION 1, CHAPTER 2 – WHAT TO SAY

2. **(Answer: C)** A distress call begins with the word "MAYDAY" spoken three times.

FURTHER READING: APM VOLUME 7, SECTION 3, CHAPTER 8 – EMERGENCY PROCEDURES

3. **(Answer: C)** ATSUs participating in the LARS are able to provide either a Traffic Service or a Deconfliction Service; both are available at the request of the pilot. The controller will inform pilots when they are receiving either a Radar Control Service (within controlled airspace), Traffic Service or Deconfliction Service (outside controlled airspace); and also whenever the level of service changes or terminates. The type of radar service being provided is information that should be read back by the pilot.

FURTHER READING: APM VOLUME 7, SECTION 2, CHAPTER 6 – R/T IN UNCONTROLLED AIRSPACE

4. **(Answer: B)** The phrase "take-off" may only be used by a pilot to acknowledge take-off clearance. At all other times the word "departure" must be used.

FURTHER READING: APM VOLUME 7, SECTION 1, CHAPTER 2 – WHAT TO SAY

5. **(Answer: C)** Height is defined as the vertical distance of a level, point or object considered as a point measured from a specified datum. The datum is normally the highest point on the landing area. With QFE set the aircraft altimeter will indicate height above the aerodrome.

    The phraseology used when referring to vertical position differs depending on the pressure setting in use:

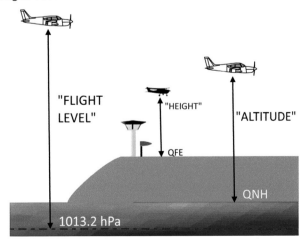

FURTHER READING: APM VOLUME 7, SECTION 1, CHAPTER 3 – AERODROME OPERATIONS

6.   **(Answer: C)** The Aeronautical Mobile Service handles messages in the following order of priority:

MESSAGE CATEGORY & ORDER OF PRIORITY	RT SIGNAL
1. Distress Calls, Distress Messages and Distress Traffic	**MAYDAY**
2. Urgency Messages	**PAN PAN**
3. Communications relating to Direction Finding (VDF).	
4. Flight Safety Messages.	
5. Meteorological Messages.	
6. Flight regularity Messages	

FURTHER READING: APM VOLUME 7, SECTION 1, CHAPTER 3 – AERODROME OPERATIONS

7.   **(Answer: B)** Flight Information Service at aerodromes is provided for the safe and efficient conduct of flights in the Aerodrome Traffic Zone. From this information pilots will be able to decide the appropriate course of action to be taken to ensure the safety of flight, i.e. the onus is on you, the pilot, to decide. The service is easily identifiable by the call sign suffix "Information".

FURTHER READING: APM VOLUME 7, SECTION 1, CHAPTER 3 – AERODROME OPERATIONS

8.   **(Answer: D)** The correct RTF phraseology format to use when requesting a QDM, is:

"(Full aircraft call sign) request QDM (full aircraft call sign)"
For example "G-MACK request QDM G-MACK"

FURTHER READING: APM VOLUME 7, SECTION 2, CHAPTER 6 – R/T IN UNCONTROLLED AIRSPACE

9.   **(Answer: B)** The Traffic Service is a surveillance (radar) based ATS where in addition to a Basic Service:

- *The controller provides specific radar derived traffic information to assist a pilot in avoiding other traffic.*
- *The service is available to IFR or VFR flights at the request of the pilot.*
- *Relevant Traffic Information will be passed and will be updated if the traffic continues to constitute a definite hazard, or if requested by the pilot.*
- *Traffic avoidance is ultimately the pilot's responsibility. Whether Traffic Information has been passed or not, a pilot is still responsible for collision avoidance.*

FURTHER READING: APM VOLUME 7, SECTION 2, CHAPTER 5 – AIRSPACE CLASSIFICATION

10.   **(Answer: C)** When instructed by an ATS Unit to "Pass your message", your reply should contain the following information, ideally in the order specified. ADDPAR is a mnemonic that may be used to keep the details in the correct order until the call becomes second nature:

A	Aircraft Call sign and Type
D	Departure Point
D	Destination
P	Present Position
A	Altitude/Level
R	Request, intentions or additional details (e.g. Flight Rules, Next route point, request–whatever is applicable to the flight)

This call format is appropriate for giving your flight details in many situations including rejoin, obtaining a radar service or basic service, requesting transit of a MATZ or permission to enter a Control Zone.

FURTHER READING: APM VOLUME 7, SECTION 1, CHAPTER 3 — AERODROME OPERATIONS

11. **(Answer: B)** The VHF band extends from 30 to 300 MHz and the range is limited by line of sight.

BAND	FREQUENCY	WAVELENGTH
VLF	3 KHz – 30 KHz	100,000 -10,000 metres
LF	30 KHz – 300 KHz	10,000 – 1000 metres
MF	300 KHz – 3 MHz	1000 – 100 metres
HF	3 MHz – 30 MHz	100 – 10 metres
VHF	**30 MHz –300 MHz**	**10 – 1 metre**
UHF	300 MHz – 3000 MHz	1 metre – 10 cm
SHF	3000 MHz – 30,000 MHz	10 cm – 1 cm

FURTHER READING: APM VOLUME 7, SECTION 5, CHAPTER 13 — RADIO WAVE PROPAGATION & LONG RANGE COMMS.

12. **(Answer: C)** Civilian traffic wishing to penetrate a MATZ should make contact with the military controller 15 nm or 5 minutes flying time before reaching the zone boundary, whichever is sooner. On the initial call to the military controller the phrase "Request MATZ penetration" must be used. For example: "Cottesmore Zone G-MORG request MATZ penetration".

FURTHER READING: APM VOLUME 7, SECTION 2, CHAPTER 6 — R/T IN UNCONTROLLED AIRSPACE

13. **(Answer: A)** A pilot in an emergency should report his/her position as: Present (or last known) Position; altitude/flight level; and heading. See the full "Mayday" call in the explanation to Question 10 of paper 3.

FURTHER READING: APM VOLUME 7, SECTION 3, CHAPTER 8 — EMERGENCY PROCEDURES

14. **(Answer: C)** Air/ Ground stations use the call sign suffix "RADIO"

UNIT	CALL SIGN	SERVICE
Area control centre	CONTROL	ATC
Radar (general)	RADAR	ATC
Approach control	APPROACH	ATC
Approach control radar arrivals	ARRIVAL/DIRECTOR	ATC
Approach control radar departures	DEPARTURE	ATC
Aerodrome control	TOWER	ATC
Surface movement control	GROUND	ATC
Flight information service	INFORMATION	FISO
Air/Ground Communication	RADIO	A/G

FURTHER READING: APM VOLUME 7, SECTION 1, CHAPTER 3 — AERODROME OPERATIONS

15. **(Answer: A)** A QDR is the magnetic bearing of the aircraft from the station.

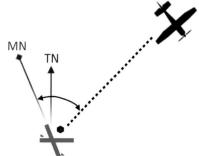

Other VDF bearings available:	
QDM	**Magnetic** heading to steer to reach the station (assuming nil wind)
QTE	Aircraft's **true** bearing from the station
QUJ	Aircraft's **true** track to the station

FURTHER READING: APM VOLUME 7, SECTION 2, CHAPTER 6 – R/T IN UNCONTROLLED AIRSPACE

16. **(Answer: B)** When a pilot is responsible for activating a flight plan, this may be done by asking an ATSU by radio to activate the flight plan.

G-POPS, departed Weston at 44, request activate flight plan

Any appropriate frequency may be used for this purpose. However, when *filing* a flight plan in the air busy frequencies should be avoided, and usually a FIS frequency is used for this purpose.

FURTHER READING: APM VOLUME 7, SECTION 1, CHAPTER 3 –AERODROME OPERATIONS

17. **(Answer: B)** CAP 413 gives the response "roger G-BH" in response to the transmission "land at your discretion". Practically it may add to the situational awareness of other pilots if you report your intentions, i.e. to land, continue or make a missed approach.

FURTHER READING: APM VOLUME 7, SECTION 1, CHAPTER 3 – AERODROME OPERATIONS

18. **(Answer: C)** The word "hectopascals" must be used when transmitting all pressure settings below 1000 e.g. QNH 994 hectopascals, QFE 987 hectopascals. This is to avoid any confusion with inches of mercury, the datum used in the United States.

FURTHER READING: APM VOLUME 7, SECTION 1, CHAPTER 4 – AERODROME INFORMATION

19. **(Answer: D)** VOLMET provides meteorological reports for certain aerodromes and are broadcast on specified frequencies. Full details can be found in the UKAIP GEN 3.5, below is an extract by way of example:

> **London (South)   128.60   H24   Continuous**
> Actual weather and forecast trend for:
> Birmingham, Bournemouth, Bristol, Cardiff, Jersey, Luton, Norwich, Southampton, Southend.
>
> **London (North)   126.60   H24   Continuous**
> Actual weather and forecast trend for:
> Blackpool, East Midlands, Leeds/Bradford, Liverpool, London/Gatwick, Manchester, Newcastle, Isle of Man/Ronaldsway, Teesside.

FURTHER READING: APM VOLUME 7, SECTION 1, CHAPTER 4 – AERODROME INFORMATION

20. **(Answer: A)** To reply to an instruction from the ground first repeat the information, read back or acknowledge the instruction, then say the aircraft call sign.

Example: **Descend to altitude three thousand feet Golf-Alpha Victor**

FURTHER READING: APM VOLUME 7, SECTION 1, CHAPTER 3 – AERODROME OPERATIONS

END OF EXPLANATIONS PAPER 4

COMMUNICATIONS PAPER 5

1. The correct pronunciation for transmitting an altitude of 2500 is:

   a. Two fife zero zero

   b. Two fife hundred

   c. Too tousand fife hundred

   d. Too fife zero zero

2. The transponder should be set to which code in the event of an emergency?

   a. 7000

   b. 7500

   c. 7600

   d. 7700

3. A ground station using the suffix "Radio" or "Information" will not use the phrase:

   a. Cleared

   b. Report

   c. Pass your message

   d. Negative

4. The time 1130 is pronounced as:

   a. Eleven thirty

   b. Wun wun tree zero, or tree zero

   c. One one three zero, or three zero

   d. Half past eleven

5. The word or phrase used to indicate that you have received an ATC message and will comply with it , is:

   a. Roger

   b. Affirm

   c. Yes

   d. Wilco

6. What does "ATIS" stand for?

   a. Aeronautical Traffic Information Service

   b. Automatic Terminal Information Service

   c. Air Traffic Information Service

   d. Airport Terminal Information Service

7. When may a pilot abbreviate the aircraft RTF call sign?

   a. Only when it has first been abbreviated by the ground station

   b. On the second call to a ground station

   c. When there will be no confusion

   d. If agreed with the ground station before flight

8. The correct content and order of a position report is:

   a. A/c call sign, position, time, level, next position and ETA

   b. A/c call sign, route, position, heading and level

   c. Position, heading, route and ETA

   d. Position, level, next position and ETA

9. The instruction "SQUAWK ALTITUDE" means:

   a. Press the IDENT button

   b. Set the transponder to standby

   c. Set the transponder to ON

   d. Set the transponder to ALT

10. In the Pooley's Flight Guide you read that WESTON, your intended destination, has a Flight Information Service. When addressing WESTON what call sign should you use?

    a. WESTON RADAR

    b. WESTON RADIO

    c. WESTON TOWER

    d. WESTON INFORMATION

11. A pilot is given an ATC instruction with which he/she cannot comply. ATC should be advised:

    a. Standby

    b. Cannot comply

    c. Unable to comply

    d. Will not comply

12. A pilot already in communication with either a civil or military ATSU on being confronted with an emergency the pilot should:

    a. Make a distress call on the frequency in use and keep any allocated squawk

    b. Select 7700 and change to 121.5 MHz

    c. Select 7000 and change to 121.5 MHz

    d. Make a distress call on 121.5 MHz and keep any allocated squawk

13. On hearing a distress message a pilot should:

    a. Immediately attempt to relay

    b. Maintain radio silence

    c. Change frequency

    d. Request a frequency change from ATC

14. You are departing an airfield. The ground station is using the call sign suffix "INFORMATION" and tells you: "G-BH Take-off at your discretion, surface wind 300/8". A suitable reply is:

    a. My discretion, surface wind 300/8 G-BH

    b. Cleared for take-off G-BH

    c. Roger G-BH

    d. Taking-off G-BH

15. Two way communication has been established with a ground station, however several of your transmissions have now gone unanswered and you suspect communication failure. What are your initial actions?

    a. Immediately divert to the nearest airfield suitable for a non-radio arrival

    b. Check that the correct frequency is still selected, confirm that the ATSU remains open, confirm that the aircraft is within range and check the receiver volume

    c. Switch to 121.5 and make blind urgency transmissions

    d. Squawk 7600, change headsets and transmit blind

16. LARS is an ATS surveillance service available to assist pilots flying outside controlled airspace. It is provided up to and including FL.... normally within ...nm of the nominated unit. The service provided will be ..... or .....::

    a. FL 85, 30 nm. Traffic service, Procedural service

    b. FL 95 40 nm. Procedural service, Deconfliction service

    c. FL 95, 30 nm. Traffic service, Deconfliction service

    d. FL 85, 40 nm. Basic service, Traffic service

17. You hear a distress call on the frequency you are working, however it remains unacknowledged by the ATSU. What action should you take?

a. Squawk 7700, change to 121.5 MHz and repeat the message exactly as heard

b. Repeat the message exactly as heard and wait for the ATSU to advise what to do

c. Relay the emergency message on the frequency currently in use, making it clear that it is not you experiencing difficulties

d. Remain silent, but continue to monitor the frequency

18. The states of emergency are:

a. Mayday and pan pan

b. Difficulty and urgency

c. Distress and urgency

d. Mayday and distress

19. Pilots requesting a MATZ crossing should pass the following information when asked to do so by the military controller:

a. Aircraft type, intention, departure and destination, route, POB

b. A/c call sign, present position, next turning point, altitude

c. A/c call sign, altitude, position, departure and destination, POB

d. A/c call sign and type, departure point and destination, present position, altitude, request or intention

20. The "student" prefix is to:

a. Advise controllers about flights operating for the purposes of flight training

b. Advise controllers and other airspace users about student pilots flying solo

c. Advise controllers and other airspace users about a flight test being undertaken

d. Advise airspace users when a first solo is taking place

END OF COMMUNICATIONS PAPER 5

No.	A	B	C	D
1			X	
2				X
3	X			
4		X		
5				X
6		X		
7	X			
8	X			
9				X
10				X
11			X	
12	X			
13		X		
14				X
15		X		
16			X	
17			X	
18			X	
19				X
20		X		

CORRECT ANSWERS: PERCENTAGES					
15	16	17	18	19	20
75%	80%	85%	90%	95%	100%

COMMUNICATIONS PAPER 5: EXPLANATIONS

Numeral or Numeral Element	Pronounciation
0	ZERO
1	WUN
2	TOO
3	TREE
4	FOW ER
5	FIFE
6	SIX
7	SEV EN
8	AIT
9	NIN ER
DECIMAL	DAYSEEMAL
HUNDRED	HUNDRED
THOUSAND	TOUSAND

1. **(Answer: C)** Altitude 2500 is pronounced **"too tousand fife hundred".**

    When transmitting altitude, height, cloud height, visibility and runway visual range (basically anything measured in feet or metres!) whole hundreds and thousands are transmitted by stating the number of hundreds and thousands followed by the word "HUN-dred" or "TOU-SAND" as applicable. Combinations follow the same rule.

    FURTHER READING: APM VOLUME 7, SECTION 1, CHAPTER 2 – WHAT TO SAY

2. **(Answer: D)** An emergency is indicated by the transponder code 7700. The following special purpose codes are in use:

    7700: Emergency
    7600: Communications failure
    7500: Unlawful interference (hijack)
    7000: UK conspicuity code
    2000: Entering an FIR, when operating under VFR, from an adjacent region where the operation of transponders has not been required.

    FURTHER READING: APM VOLUME 7, SECTION 1, CHAPTER 1 – COCKPIT RADIOS

3. **(Answer: A)** The word "cleared" will only be used by used by an Air Traffic Control Officer, since only an ATCO can issue a clearance. An ATC service is denoted by several call sign suffixes each related to the function being carried out. The ones most likely to be encountered are: "Radar", "Approach", "Tower", "Ground" or "Control".

    FURTHER READING: APM VOLUME 7, SECTION 1, CHAPTER 3 – AERODROME OPERATIONS

4. **(Answer: B)** Note you are asked for the pronunciation, 1130 is spoken as "wun wun tree zero" or "tree zero". Normally when transmitting time only the minutes of the hour are required. If there is a possibility of confusion the hour should be included as well.

Time	Transmitted as:	Pronounced as:
0805	ZERO FIVE (or zero eight zero five)	ZERO FIFE
1300	ONE THREE ZERO ZERO	WUN TREE ZERO ZERO
2258	FIVE EIGHT (or two two five eight)	FIFE AIT

    FURTHER READING: APM VOLUME 7, SECTION 1, CHAPTER 2 – WHAT TO SAY

5. **(Answer: D)** Wilco means: I understand your message and will comply with it (a contraction of "will comply").

    FURTHER READING: APM VOLUME 7, SECTION 1, CHAPTER 3 – AERODROME OPERATIONS

6. **(Answer: B)** ATIS, Automatic Terminal Information Service. At busier airports an Automatic Terminal Information Service is broadcast to provide a range of data, usually weather conditions and essential aerodrome information, on a discreet frequency or selected VOR. Each ATIS message is coded consecutively using the phonetic alphabet. A new message is generated at regular intervals (usually half hourly at the time of the routine meteorological observations at minutes 20 and 50) or whenever a significant change occurs. Pilots should advise ATC that they have received the latest ATIS:

    On Departure – before taxiing
    On Arrival – on first contact with the ATSU.

    FURTHER READING: APM VOLUME 7, SECTION 1, CHAPTER 4 – AERODROME INFORMATION

7. **(Answer: A)** Once satisfactory communication is established, and provided that no confusion is likely, the call sign may be abbreviated. The pilot of an aircraft may only abbreviate the call sign if the relevant aeronautical ground station has abbreviated it first.

FURTHER READING: APM VOLUME 7, SECTION 1, CHAPTER 3 – AERODROME OPERATIONS

8. **(Answer: A)** The standard format for a position report is:

A	Aircraft call sign
P	Position
T	Time
L	Level
N	Next reporting point
E	ETA for the next reporting point

For example: Golf Hotel Bravo Alpha Hotel overhead Bromham 24, estimate Barkway at 46

FURTHER READING: APM VOLUME 7, SECTION 2, CHAPTER 5 – AIRSPACE CLASSIFICATION

9. **(Answer: D)** "Squawk Altitude" means select the ALT setting on the transponder

TRANSPONDER MODE SELECTION	
OFF	The transponder is totally off
STANDBY	The transponder is ready for use but not actually transmitting
ON	The transponder will reply to an interrogation signal, using the four-digit code set in the control panel.
ALT	As for "ON", plus your altitude or flight level will also be displayed on the controller's radar screen.
IDENT	If a controller asks you to squawk "ident" you should press the ident button. This causes a flashing circle to appear around your aircraft's radar return. "Ident" is also known as the SPI (special position identification) feature.

FURTHER READING: APM VOLUME 7, SECTION 1, CHAPTER 1 – COCKPIT RADIOS

10. **(Answer: D)** A Flight Information Service at an aerodrome uses the call sign suffix "INFORMATION".

FURTHER READING: APM VOLUME 7, SECTION 1, CHAPTER 3 – AERODROME OPERATIONS

11. **(Answer: C)** "UNABLE TO COMPLY" is the phrase to use when you are given an ATC instruction which you cannot carry out.

FURTHER READING: APM VOLUME 7, SECTION 1, CHAPTER 3 – AERODROME OPERATIONS

12. **(Answer: A)** The first attempt to transmit an emergency message should be made on the frequency currently in use. If this is not successful the pilot should transmit his/her intention is to change to the Aeronautical Emergency Frequency 121.5 MHz.

A pilot already in communication with a civil or military ATSU should maintain any SSR code setting previously assigned by ATC (other than the Conspicuity Code 7000) until instructions are received to change the code setting.

FURTHER READING: APM VOLUME 7, SECTION 3, CHAPTER 8 – EMERGENCY PROCEDURES

13. **(Answer: B)** Transmissions from aircraft in distress have priority over all other transmissions. On hearing a distress call, all stations must maintain radio silence on that frequency unless:

- The distress is cancelled or the distress traffic is terminated;
- The distress traffic has been transferred to another frequency;
- The station controlling communications gives permission; or
- The station itself has to render assistance.

FURTHER READING: APM VOLUME 7, SECTION 3, CHAPTER 8 – EMERGENCY PROCEDURES

14. **(Answer: D)** In response to the transmission "take-off at your discretion" you are required to notify the FISO of your intentions; hence "Taking-off G-BH".

As you can see, on departure we are REQUIRED to advise the FISO of our intentions. However, on landing CAP 413 details that the response to "land at your discretion" is simply "Roger" followed by your call sign. Practically it may add to the situational awareness of other pilots if you report your intentions, i.e. to land, continue or make a missed approach.

FURTHER READING: APM VOLUME 7, SECTION 1, CHAPTER 3 – AERODROME OPERATIONS

15. **(Answer: B)** Should a radio failure be suspected the following actions are recommended:
Initial Actions, check that:

1. The correct frequency has been selected.
2. The aeronautical station being called is actually open.
3. The aircraft is within radio range - remember that VHF is line of sight only.
4. The receiver volume is at a suitable level.
5. Headsets are plugged in correctly and serviceable (try a spare headset or hand microphone).
6. The radio installation is set correctly, perhaps try a second "box", check the fuses, squelch.

Subsequent Actions:

7. Attempt to contact on another frequency appropriate to the route.
8. Attempt to establish communication with other aircraft.
9. Transmit Blind, including the name of the station being addressed, in case the transmitter is serviceable. A blind transmission should be made twice.
10. Listen out on the designated frequency, it may be possible to use the speechless code if the problem is just a transmitter failure

FURTHER READING: APM VOLUME 7, SECTION 3, CHAPTER 9 – RADIO FAILURE PROCEDURES

16. **(Answer: C)** Outside Controlled Airspace certain Air Traffic units are able to provide a Lower Airspace Radar Service to pilots flying in UK uncontrolled airspace up to and including FL 95, within approximately 30nm of each participating unit. Participating ATCUs are able to provide either a Traffic Service or a Deconfliction Service; both are available at the request of the pilot. The controller will inform pilots when they are receiving either a Radar Control, Traffic or Deconfliction service; and also whenever the level of service changes, this information should be read back by the pilot.

FURTHER READING: APM VOLUME 7, SECTION 2, CHAPTER 6 – R/T IN UNCONTROLLED AIRSPACE

17. **(Answer: C)** Where a distress call is made which goes unacknowledged by ATC, any station hearing the call should assume responsibility for ensuring that the message is passed. It could be that the aircraft in trouble is already too low for the signal to reach the ground station, remember that VHF is line of sight only. The most important thing is to make it clear that the aircraft transmitting is not itself in distress. Below is an example of the phraseology to use:

MAYDAY, MAYDAY, MAYDAY. Colney Radar, G-MEME **has intercepted mayday from G-BUGA, I say again, G-BUGA,** Cherokee, engine failure, landing in a field 15 miles north of Weston, heading 340 degrees, altitude 2,500 feet, PPL, 2 POB.

FURTHER READING: APM VOLUME 7, SECTION 3, CHAPTER 8 – EMERGENCY PROCEDURES

18. **(Answer: C)** Distress and urgency are two states of emergency. They are defined as:

DISTRESS is a condition of being threatened by grave and/or imminent danger and of requiring immediate assistance. A distress message will take priority over all other messages.

URGENCY is a condition concerning the safety of an aircraft or other vehicle, or of some other person on board or within sight, but not requiring immediate assistance.

FURTHER READING: APM VOLUME 7, SECTION 3, CHAPTER 8 – EMERGENCY PROCEDURES

19. **(Answer: D)** When instructed an ATS Unit to "Pass your message", your reply should contain the following information, ideally in the order specified. ADDPAR is a mnemonic that may be used to keep the details in the correct order:

A	Aircraft call sign and type
D	Departure point
D	Destination
P	Present Position
A	Altitude/Level
R	Request, intentions or additional details (eg. flight rules, next route point, request–whatever is applicable to the flight)

This call format is appropriate for giving your flight details in many situations including rejoin, obtaining a radar service or basic service, requesting transit of a MATZ or permission to enter a Control Zone.

FURTHER READING: APM VOLUME 7, SECTION 1, CHAPTER 3 – AERODROME OPERATIONS

20. **(Answer: B)** The student prefix is used to advise controllers and other airspace users about student pilots flying solo.

On initial contact with a new ATSU, student pilots who are flying solo shall use the call sign prefix 'STUDENT'. Controllers will acknowledge the initial call, repeating the prefix, and will try to make allowance for the limited experience and ability of student pilots. Especially in determining the pace and complexity of instructions and/or information which are passed.

FURTHER READING: APM VOLUME 7, SECTION 1, CHAPTER 3 – AERODROME OPERATIONS

END OF EXPLANATIONS PAPER 5

Additional Blank Answer Sheets 51 - 54

INTENTIONALLY BLANK

ANSWER SHEETS

PAPER NO.				
	A	B	C	D
1				
2				
3				
4				
5				
6				
7				
8				
9				
10				
11				
12				
13				
14				
15				
16				
17				
18				
19				
20				

PAPER NO.				
	A	B	C	D
1				
2				
3				
4				
5				
6				
7				
8				
9				
10				
11				
12				
13				
14				
15				
16				
17				
18				
19				
20				

PAPER NO.				
	A	B	C	D
1				
2				
3				
4				
5				
6				
7				
8				
9				
10				
11				
12				
13				
14				
15				
16				
17				
18				
19				
20				

PAPER NO.				
	A	B	C	D
1				
2				
3				
4				
5				
6				
7				
8				
9				
10				
11				
12				
13				
14				
15				
16				
17				
18				
19				
20				

PAPER NO.				
	A	B	C	D
1				
2				
3				
4				
5				
6				
7				
8				
9				
10				
11				
12				
13				
14				
15				
16				
17				
18				
19				
20				

PAPER NO.				
	A	B	C	D
1				
2				
3				
4				
5				
6				
7				
8				
9				
10				
11				
12				
13				
14				
15				
16				
17				
18				
19				
20				

PAPER NO.				
	A	B	C	D
1				
2				
3				
4				
5				
6				
7				
8				
9				
10				
11				
12				
13				
14				
15				
16				
17				
18				
19				
20				

PAPER NO.				
	A	B	C	D
1				
2				
3				
4				
5				
6				
7				
8				
9				
10				
11				
12				
13				
14				
15				
16				
17				
18				
19				
20				

PAPER NO.				
	A	B	C	D
1				
2				
3				
4				
5				
6				
7				
8				
9				
10				
11				
12				
13				
14				
15				
16				
17				
18				
19				
20				

PAPER NO.				
	A	B	C	D
1				
2				
3				
4				
5				
6				
7				
8				
9				
10				
11				
12				
13				
14				
15				
16				
17				
18				
19				
20				

PAPER NO.				
	A	B	C	D
1				
2				
3				
4				
5				
6				
7				
8				
9				
10				
11				
12				
13				
14				
15				
16				
17				
18				
19				
20				

PAPER NO.				
	A	B	C	D
1				
2				
3				
4				
5				
6				
7				
8				
9				
10				
11				
12				
13				
14				
15				
16				
17				
18				
19				
20				